P9-BBP-715

Shattering Earthquakes

Heinemann Library
Chicago, Illinois

Louise and Richard Spilsbury

© 2004 Heinemann Library
a division of Reed Elsevier Inc.
Chicago, Illinois

Customer Service   888–454–2279
Visit our website at www.heinemannlibrary.com

Designed by David Poole and Paul Myerscough
Illustrations by Geoff Ward
Originated by Dot Gradations Limited
Printed in China by Wing King Tong

07 06 05 04 03
10 9 8 7 6 5 4 3 2 1

Library of Congress Cataloging-in-Publication Data
Spilsbury, Louise.
   Shattering earthquakes / Louise and Richard Spilsbury.
      v. cm. -- (Awesome forces of nature)
Includes bibliographical references and index.
Contents: What is an earthquake? -- What causes earthquakes? -- Where do earthquakes happen? -- West Midlands, 2002 -- What happens in an earthquake? -- San Francisco, USA, 1989 -- Who helps after an earthquake? -- Iran, 1990 -- Can earthquakes be predicted? -- Can people prepare for earthquakes? -- Can earthquakes be prevented? -- Earthquakes of the past.
   ISBN 1-4034-4784-5 (lib. bdg.) -- ISBN 1-4034-5446-9 (pbk.)
   1. Earthquakes--Juvenile literature. [1. Earthquakes.] I. Spilsbury, Richard, 1963- II. Title.
   QE521.3.S657 2003
   551.22--dc21

                              2003011619

Acknowledgments
The author and publisher are grateful to the following for permission to reproduce copyright material:
Cover photograph by Wally Santana/Associated Press.
p.4 Eric Risberg/AP; pp.5, 13 Sipa Press/Rex Features; p.7 Kevin Schafer/Still Pictures; p.8 Leonette Medici, Stringer/AP; pp.9, 12, 15, 17 National Geophysical Data Center, Boulder, Colorado/NOAA; p.11 British Geological Survey; pp.14, 15, 16 Paul Sakuma/AP; p.18 Oxford Scientific Films; p.19 John Swart/AP; pp.20, 21, 24 Sten Rosenlund/Rex Features; p.22 Ian McKain/AP; pp.23, 26 Roger Ressmeyer/Corbis; p.25 Galen Rowell/Corbis; p.27 David Parker/Science Photo Library; p.28 FEMA.

Some words are shown in bold, **like this.** You can find out what they mean by looking in the glossary.

3 1967 00853 4375

Contents

What Is an Earthquake?

Imagine you are reading at a table. You notice that the clock on the table is beginning to wobble. Then you hear a rumbling sound, like an airplane flying above the house. Objects in the room rattle and shake more and more. Suddenly the whole room jerks, knocking things off the table and pictures off the walls.

This is how it can feel in an earthquake. An earthquake happens when Earth's surface moves. The ground under our feet usually feels solid, but during an earthquake it shakes, cracks open, and dips. Most earthquakes are very small, and people may only feel a slight trembling under their feet. Other earthquakes can make cracks in walls and shake books off shelves. The worst earthquakes in the world can cause terrible destruction.

Rescue dogs were used to search for survivors after a 1989 earthquake destroyed these buildings in San Francisco, California.

Large earthquakes can transform huge areas of land in an instant. During a major earthquake, the shaking of the ground can knock down buildings, break open roads, and make huge cracks appear in the land. Cars, buildings, and whole lakes can disappear into these cracks.

EARTHQUAKE ⚡ FACTS

! Earthquakes cause more damage than any other kind of natural **disaster.**

! Several million earthquakes happen around the world each year. Most are so weak that people cannot even feel them.

! Most earthquakes last for less than a minute, but people can often feel them over a huge area.

The huge cracks in this road were caused by a strong earthquake in Gujarat, India.

What Causes Earthquakes?

Earthquakes are movements of the ground. They usually happen in certain places because of Earth's structure. To understand how earthquakes happen, you need to know about the structure of our planet.

The surface of Earth is made of a layer of hard rock. This layer forms the land and the floor of the oceans. It is called the **crust.** Under the crust, there is more rock. Millions of years ago, this rock cracked like the shell of an egg. It split into giant pieces called **plates.** These plates float like huge rafts on hot, liquid rock deep inside Earth. They move very, very slowly.

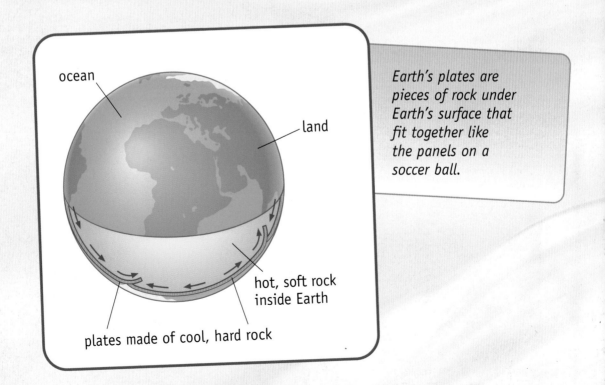

ocean

land

hot, soft rock inside Earth

plates made of cool, hard rock

Earth's plates are pieces of rock under Earth's surface that fit together like the panels on a soccer ball.

Moving plates

As the plates move, they rub or slide against each other. The place where plates meet is called a **fault.** In most places, one plate slides against another in a slow and steady way. Most plates move at a speed of only an inch or two each year—about as fast as your fingernails grow.

Sometimes two plates get stuck against each other. For many years, they slowly push harder and harder against each other. Suddenly the force becomes too great and these gigantic plates of rock slip past each other. When this happens, the crust shudders and shakes. This shaking is an earthquake. The force of the plates moving can open cracks in the crust above and around the fault.

Fault lines are usually deep underground, but some can be seen on the surface. This is the San Andreas Fault. It runs down the west coast of North America.

Shock waves

The point on Earth's surface above the start of an earthquake is called the **epicenter.** The force of an earthquake spreads out in all directions from the epicenter. These movements are called **shock waves.** Shock waves travel through the rocks around the epicenter like ripples on a pond when you throw in a stone. Shock waves can travel for hundreds of miles, but they become weaker as they travel away from the epicenter.

Aftershocks

Earthquakes usually happen in groups. A major earthquake may start off with small earth **tremors** that gradually get stronger. These tremors may happen several days before the main earthquake happens. After the main earthquake, there may be **aftershocks.** Many aftershocks are too small to feel, but others are like smaller earthquakes. They usually occur within a few days, getting weaker over time.

This damage in Umbria, Italy, was not caused by a main earthquake. It was caused by the aftershocks that followed an earthquake in 1997.

Measuring earthquakes

Earthquakes are measured on the **Richter scale.** This scale is based on the amount of damage earthquakes cause. The weakest earthquake is rated 1 and the strongest earthquake possible would be rated 10.

What do the ratings mean?

- Rating 2.0 or below: small earthquake that cannot be felt by people and is not recorded

- Below 4.0: earthquake that can be felt but usually causes little or no damage

- Over 5.0: earthquake that is felt by all and could cause some damage

- Over 6.0: earthquake that can cause serious damage to buildings

- Over 7.0: major earthquake that causes severe damage and can destroy buildings

- Over 8.0: earthquake that causes almost total destruction

On August 17, 1999, a strong earthquake shook the cities of Izmit and Istanbul in Turkey. It measured 7.4 on the Richter scale and caused terrible damage.

Where Do Earthquakes Happen?

Earthquakes can happen anywhere on land or on the ocean floor. Some earthquakes happen in the middle of **plates.** They happen in places where there is a line of weakness in Earth's **crust.** Most earthquakes, though, happen where two of Earth's plates meet.

Many earthquakes happen around the edges of the Pacific Ocean. Several plates meet there, and hot liquid rock can escape to the surface. Many earthquakes happen in this area, and **volcanoes** are also common there. This area has been named the Ring of Fire. Another area that suffers from many earthquakes is a zone that runs from Italy and Greece through central Asia and the Himalayas.

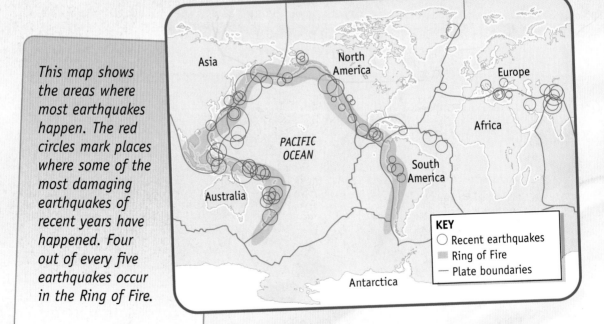

This map shows the areas where most earthquakes happen. The red circles mark places where some of the most damaging earthquakes of recent years have happened. Four out of every five earthquakes occur in the Ring of Fire.

Asia

North America

Europe

Africa

PACIFIC OCEAN

South America

Australia

Antarctica

KEY
○ Recent earthquakes
▪ Ring of Fire
— Plate boundaries

United Kingdom, 2002

Few people think of the United Kingdom as a country that has earthquakes. In fact, this country has a powerful earthquake every ten years or so. The most recent one began around 1 A.M. on September 23, 2002. Thousands of people woke up to the sounds of their furniture shaking and windows rattling. The earthquake measured 4.8 on the **Richter scale.** Its **epicenter** was in Dudley in the West Midlands. It shook buildings in parts of the West Midlands, Wales, North Yorkshire, London, and Wiltshire for up to 30 seconds.

"The house started shaking quite violently. All the power was cut off. Quite a few people came out of their houses wondering what was going on. The streets were in darkness." Richard Flynn, West Midlands

No one was hurt in the West Midlands earthquake. But there was some minor damage.

11

What Happens in an Earthquake?

Earthquakes usually do the most damage at the **epicenter.** However, **shock waves** can make land shake and tremble for miles around. In a severe earthquake, the ground can rise and fall like waves in the sea. In the worst cases, the entire shape of the land can change.

When an earthquake shakes the ground, it can make walls crack and roofs fall in. If one building falls, it can make the one next to it collapse, too. When earthquakes shake the ground, they can break **power lines** and gas pipes. Sparks from power lines can cause fires, and leaking gas can cause explosions. Earthquakes can rip apart roads and crack or bend bridges. **Aftershocks** bring even more damage. Buildings that were weakened by the first earthquake may fall down during an aftershock.

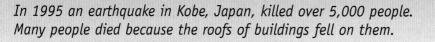

In 1995 an earthquake in Kobe, Japan, killed over 5,000 people. Many people died because the roofs of buildings fell on them.

Mexico City, 1985

Earthquakes can change the **landscape** by opening cracks in the ground and changing land levels. They can also turn solid land into soft, dangerous land.

On September 19, 1985, a huge earthquake hit Mexico City. The epicenter was 30 miles (50 kilometers) from the west coast. However, the earthquake still rated 8.1 on the **Richter scale** when it reached Mexico City, over 185 miles (300 kilometers) from the coast. The earthquake caused great damage because the city sits on soil made of soft sand and clay. The shock waves shook the soil grains, turning it into **quicksand.** This caused buildings to tilt, shift, or even sink. Over 10,000 people were killed.

Once the dust clouds had cleared, it became obvious that much of Mexico City had been reduced to rubble.

Do Earthquakes Cause Other Disasters?

Earthquakes do not just break or bury buildings, bridges, and roads. They can also set off other **disasters** such as **landslides.** When a hill is damaged by an earthquake, the soil on the side of the hill can slide down. When large amounts of sand or soil fall like this, people or buildings can be buried at the bottom of the hill.

The town beneath the sea

In 1692 an earthquake started a landslide in a town called Port Royal on the island of Jamaica. The whole town slid into the sea and became buried in the **seafloor.** It was not until 1959 that divers found objects from this lost city on the seafloor.

In 2001 an earthquake rocked El Salvador. It caused a landslide that buried the small town of Las Colinas. The landslide buried hundreds of houses and killed 315 people.

Earthquakes under the sea

Earthquakes do not only happen on land. They also happen on the seafloor. When an earthquake happens deep under the water, it creates a giant wave called a **tsunami.** Most tsunamis are barely noticeable in the deep parts of oceans. But they get bigger as they approach land. When a tsunami hits a coastline, it can become a huge wall of water. It will sweep away, crush, or flood anything in its path.

The strongest earthquake ever recorded measured 9.5 on the **Richter scale.** It struck on May 22, 1960, off the coast of southern Chile. It created a tsunami that caused great destruction in Chile, Hawaii, and Japan.

In July 1998 a tsunami struck Sissano in northern Papua New Guinea. Many houses were swept away by the water, and thousands of people were injured or killed.

San Francisco, 1989

The city of San Francisco lies on the San Andreas **Fault** and has had several huge earthquakes in the past. On October 17, 1989, another strong earthquake hit the city. The **epicenter** was near Santa Cruz, but the earthquake also affected San Francisco and Oakland, 50 miles (80 kilometers) away.

It was early evening—around 5 P.M.—and San Francisco was busy. Many fans were in the city's baseball stadium. They were getting ready to watch a World Series game. Workers were on their way home. The earthquake lasted less than 20 seconds and rated 7.1 on the **Richter scale.** It killed about 60 people, injured more than 3,000 people, and caused about $10 billion worth of damage.

The top level of this highway collapsed onto the lower level during the 1989 San Francisco earthquake. Cars were crushed, 42 people were killed, and 200 people were injured.

U.S.

San Francisco
Oakland
✕ epicenter
Santa Cruz

CALIFORNIA

PACIFIC
OCEAN

Different kinds of damage

There were scenes of destruction throughout northern California. In the Santa Cruz Mountains, a building slid all the way down a hillside. The earthquake also created cracks in a mountainside. One person who lived in the mountains said, "I can't stop shaking. I guess I'm surviving, but I'm scared."

Many roads were cracked or split. **Landslides** and **rock slides** blocked others. Over 90 bridges in the area were damaged, and San Francisco's Bay Bridge was closed for months. Many **mobile homes**, buildings, and businesses were destroyed. Other buildings buckled and bent. The earthquake cracked gas pipes, which led to fires in one area. Water pipes were also damaged, so firefighters had to pump water from San Francisco Bay to put out the fires.

The San Francisco earthquake caused huge land movements. This building fell onto a car that was parked in the street.

Who Helps After an Earthquake?

Most earthquakes are over in a matter of seconds, but they can cause terrible damage and destruction. The first job after a major earthquake is to rescue survivors and prevent other **disasters** from causing further damage.

Rescue workers

Firefighters, the army, and **volunteers** all work to rescue people trapped in their homes or cars. Rescue workers may use specially trained dogs that can find people by sniffing them out. Often, rescue workers use lifting and cutting equipment to get people out from under crushed buildings or fallen bridges. Damage to buildings and roads after an earthquake may make emergency work more difficult. For example, blocked roads keep firefighters from reaching fires. Construction workers may have to bring cranes and power shovels to clear the roads first. Rescue work is very dangerous because **aftershocks** can continue to happen.

This French rescue team is searching for survivors after an earthquake in India. Their dogs can smell people trapped under the rubble.

Helping people

Ambulances try to arrive at the scene as quickly as possible. Ambulance staff give emergency medical treatment and take injured people to the hospital. Workers from the Red Cross and other **aid organizations** also help after earthquakes. As well as giving **first aid,** they provide earthquake victims with a place to stay and food to eat.

The work does not stop after everyone has been rescued or taken to the hospital. New homes have to be built for people who have lost their homes. Aid organizations help reunite people that have become separated from their families. People may have also lost their businesses or shops. Ordinary people send money to help earthquake victims rebuild their lives.

*After an earthquake workers clean up the **debris** from damaged buildings and roads. They also check to be sure that any buildings left standing are safe enough for people to live in.*

Iran, 1990

At 12:30 A.M. on June 21, 1990, an earthquake blasted through northwest Iran. It rated 7.7 on the **Richter scale** and was the worst earthquake in the country for twelve years. The earthquake killed 50,000 people, injured 200,000 more, and left half a million people homeless.

The first earthquake lasted a whole minute. Then there were twelve **aftershocks.** Whole towns and villages were destroyed. In one area, a **dam** was shaken so badly that water spilled out. The water caused floods that killed many people.

In towns like this one, every single building was flattened and almost everyone living there was killed.

Rescue operations

There was so much **debris** blocking roads that workers had to use bulldozers to clear the way for ambulances and other rescue vehicles. In areas where emergency services could not get through to help, **volunteers** used their bare hands to rescue trapped families. Other workers used cranes to lift people from piles of concrete.

The rescue workers faced many difficulties. For example, the earthquake broke a lot of underground pipes. Many areas did not have any water or electricity for days or even weeks.

*After the Iran earthquake, the Red Cross **aid organization** flew in trained medical workers and supplies by helicopter.*

Can Earthquakes Be Predicted?

It is very hard to tell when and where an earthquake will happen. Sometimes there are small **tremors** before an earthquake that cause animals to behave oddly. Dogs bark wildly, horses rear up, and snakes, mice, and rats come out of their holes. However, these things do not always happen. When they do happen, there may be too little time to escape before the earthquake begins.

Studying earthquakes

Scientists who study earthquakes are called **seismologists.** They use machines called **seismographs** to measure and record the shaking of the ground. They gather information from thousands of seismographs all around the world. Using maps of the world's **faults,** seismologists study slight movements of the ground. If there is more shaking and ground movement than usual, an earthquake is more likely.

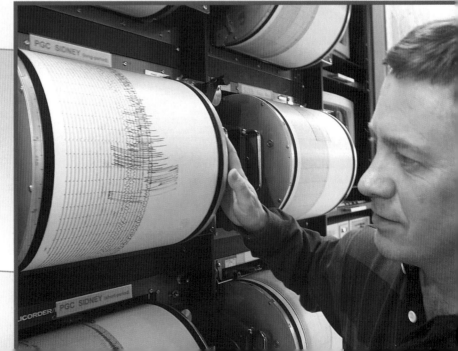

This is a chart made by a seismograph. The squiggly lines show that the ground has moved. The more the ground shakes, the larger the squiggle.

Seismographs can gather useful information about an earthquake as it happens. However, scientists are also working on ways to predict earthquakes. One way to predict earthquakes is by using information collected by **satellites.** Cameras in the satellites measure the shape of Earth's **crust.** These measurements show if there are small changes that could warn of an earthquake. Scientists hope that this information will help them predict some earthquakes in the future.

A success story

In 1975 there were several warning sings that an earthquake was about to happen in Haicheng, China. Animals were behaving oddly, land was shifting, water was seeping out of the ground, and there were weak tremors. When the tremors got stronger, people were told to **evacuate.** Many lives were saved. Unfortunately, most earthquakes do not give such clear warnings.

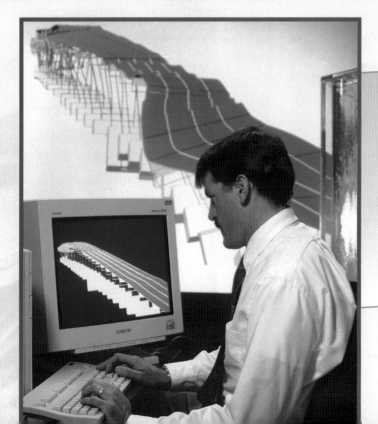

*This **engineer** is using a computer to study the effects of an earthquake on a raised highway in Oakland, California. Engineers are always trying to make highways safer in earthquake areas.*

Can People Prepare for Earthquakes?

Today it is almost impossible to predict when an earthquake will happen. The best way to reduce earthquake damage is for everyone to be well prepared.

Making buildings safer

One of the main causes of death in an earthquake is people being crushed under buildings. One of the ways to save lives is to build homes and other buildings that are strong enough to survive earthquakes. Even in the strongest earthquakes, buildings should remain standing at least long enough for people to escape. **Engineers** design buildings that can move slightly in an earthquake without breaking apart.

In the San Francisco earthquake of 1989, this building shook badly. However, the building was not damaged and no one was hurt. The 49-story office building has special supports at its base that protect it from the ground-shaking effects of earthquakes.

The most important thing engineers must consider is the land they will build on. Tall buildings should never be placed on loose soil that might sink or shift in an earthquake. When people make bridges or office buildings with metal frames, they should include rubber pads to absorb an earthquake's **shock waves.** These pads allow the building to move slightly instead of breaking apart.

What about poorer countries?

Unfortunately, many earthquakes happen in places where people cannot afford to pay for the construction of sturdy buildings. Poorer people may have no choice about the materials they use to build their homes. In Peru millions of people live in **adobe** houses. These houses are often destroyed by earthquakes because the walls are not connected together and mud is a weak building material.

One way of strengthening adobe buildings is to join the corners with a wire mesh and cover them with concrete. However, even this solution costs too much for many people.

How should people prepare?

People who live in earthquake zones should not worry about earthquakes. However, everyone in the family should learn exactly what to do in case an earthquake occurs. They should all know how to **evacuate.** They should know a safe place to go and a safe route to get there. Local government offices can give people information about what to do in an earthquake.

Things to do

There are several ways people can make their homes safer. Things that can fall, break, or start fires may injure people. People should bolt or strap gas heaters, cupboards, and bookcases to the walls so they do not tip over. It is also a good idea to keep heavy objects on bottom shelves and to hang pictures and mirrors away from beds.

This team is strengthening the basement of a house so that it will hold up better in an earthquake.

What to do in an earthquake

One way to be prepared is by knowing what to do in an earthquake. Here are some tips.

- Try not to panic. Earthquakes are scary, but they usually only last a few seconds.

- If you are inside, take cover immediately under a strong table or desk. Stay away from glass, windows, or anything that could fall, such as a bookcase.

- If you are outdoors, move away from buildings, street lights, telephone wires, and **power lines.**

- If you are in a crowded place, do not rush for the doors if everyone else is doing so. Never get into an elevator.

- Do not forget that there may be **aftershocks** following an earthquake. Aftershocks can cause things that were weakened by the main earthquake to fall down.

These students are being taught what to do in the event of an earthquake. One of the most important things to remember is to duck and cover. Get down under a desk to protect yourself from falling objects.

Can Earthquakes Be Prevented?

An earthquake is an awesome force of nature that people cannot control. Earthquakes have always happened and always will. To limit the damage earthquakes cause, people must understand the dangers. They should build or alter their homes to make them less likely to fall down when an earthquake happens.

Today scientists can only predict the general region where an earthquake might occur. They cannot be sure about when it will happen. In the future scientists hope to set up systems across the world that can more accurately predict earthquakes. With these systems they will be able to tell people to **evacuate** before an earthquake begins.

In order to reduce earthquake damage, people need to learn what earthquakes are and what to do if an earthquake happens in their area.

Major Earthquakes of the Recent Past

1976, Tangshan, China
The Chinese city of Tangshan was reduced to rubble in an earthquake that killed between 200,000 and 500,000 people.

1988, Armenia
In December 1988, an earthquake measuring 6.9 on the **Richter scale** hit northwest Armenia, killing 25,000 people.

1993, Makarashtra, India
About 10,000 villagers were killed and 65 villages were destroyed during an earthquake in southwest India in September 1993.

1995, Kobe, Japan
In January 1995, 5,500 people were killed after this earthquake.

1997, Iran
In February 1997, an earthquake measuring 5.5 on the Richter scale killed 1,000 people. Three months later a stronger **tremor** killed 1,560 more people.

1998, Afghanistan
An earthquake in northern Afghanistan killed 4,000 people on May 30, 1998.

1999, Turkey
On August 17, 1999, an earthquake measuring 7.4 on the Richter scale shook the cities of Izmit and Istanbul, killing more than 17,000 people and injuring tens of thousands more.

2001, Gujarat, India
An earthquake in Gujarat, India killed more than 20,000 people and injured more than 100,000 people.

Glossary

adobe   clay used to make bricks that are dried in the sun

aftershock   small tremor or ground movement that happens soon after the main earthquake

aid organization   group of people who work together to raise money and provide help for people in need

crust   layer of rock that forms the land and the bottoms of the oceans

dam   barrier built across a river to stop its normal flow. Dams are also used to store water in a reservoir.

debris   broken pieces of buildings, trees, rocks, etc.

disaster   event that causes damage and suffering

engineer   person who plans or designs

epicenter   point on Earth's surface above the start of an earthquake

evacuate   move away from danger until it is safe to return

fault   place where two or more plates meet below Earth's crust

first aid   first medical help given to injured people

flood   large area of water covers land that is normally dry

landscape   all the land that can be seen from one place

landslide   when a large piece of land suddenly slides down a slope

mobile home   home that can be moved

plates   sheet of rock that forms part of the surface of Earth

power line   cable that carries electricity

quicksand   loose sand into which objects can sink

Richter scale   scale that rates the amount of destruction caused by an earthquake

rock slide   tumbling of rocks down the side of a hill or mountain

satellite   object made by humans and put into space. Satellites do jobs such as sending out television signals or taking photographs.

seafloor   solid bottom of a sea or ocean

seismograph   machine that measures and records the shaking of the ground

seismologist   scientist who studies earthquakes

shock wave   movement that travels through the ground. A shock wave is caused by an earthquake.

tremor   shaking

tsunami   giant wave caused by an earthquake or landslide

volcano   opening in Earth's surface through which lava, hot gases, smoke, and ash escape

volunteer   person who offers help without being paid

More Books to Read

George, Linda. *Plate Tectonics*. Farmington Hills, Mich.:
Gale Group, 2002.

Murray, Peter. *Earthquakes*. Eden Prairie, Minn.:
Child's World, 1998.

Sherrow, Victoria. *San Francisco Earthquake, 1989: Death
and Destruction*. Berkeley Heights, N.J.: Enslow
Publishers, 1998.

Zannos, Susan. *Charles Richter and the Story of the
Richter Scale*. Bear, Del.: Mitchell Lane
Publishers, 2003.

Index